The Big Little Devotional Guide

PRAISE PARTY

Little WORSHIP Company

© The Little Worship Company Ltd 2019

With thanks to Tim Dobson, Sarah Joy, Colse Leung, Rachel Noyce, Jo Sunderland and Jenny Sykes.

Additional images by Sarah Joy, Ramsey Selim, Jo Sunderland and Shutterstock.

Scripture quotations (unless marked otherwise) taken from The Holy Bible, New International Version® Anglicized, NIV®. Copyright © 1979, 1984, 2011 by Biblica, Inc.®. Used by permission. All rights reserved worldwide.

Scriptures marked “MSG” or “The Message” taken from THE MESSAGE. Copyright © 1993, 1994, 1995, 1996, 2000, 2001, 2002. Used by permission of NavPress Publishing Group.

Scriptures marked “LWC” are original translations by The Little Worship Company (in consultation with Wycliffe Bible Translators). © The Little Worship Company Ltd 2019

Contents

Introduction 6

How to use this resource 7

Praise Party 8

Discovering GOD together

At **Little Worship Company**, our heart is to inspire and delight children with a knowledge of God, and to support them as they begin to take their first steps of faith. We also want to help parents as they walk with their children on this wonderful journey. Our range of beautifully-crafted, Biblically-based resources have been designed with the whole family in mind, so that all God's children, little ones and bigger ones, can discover more of God and His incredible love together.

There are four stunning DVDs that make up **Little Worship Company** Series 1:

- **Amazing Me**
- **Beautiful World**
- **Praise Party**
- **Wonderful Day**

This devotional guide has been written for use alongside the **Little Worship Company: Praise Party** DVD. In this book, you and your family are invited to journey with our hosts, Hal and Mr. and Mrs. Looyah, as they discover lots of different ways of praising God together.

Welcome to Praise Party!

Everyone loves a party – and the best ones of all are praise parties! **Little Worship Company: Praise Party** Devotional Guide helps us to understand what it means to praise and worship God, not only with singing, dancing and instruments, but with our hearts, feet and hands too – to keep us praising God in every season of our lives.

How to use this resource

To make the most of this resource, choose a time of the day or week which suits you and your family. It might be just before bed, just after lunch or sometime over the weekend.

- **Watch a chapter from the DVD.** Each chapter will include a short slot from Hal and a worship song.
- **Read through the accompanying Bible verse** and short, family-friendly reflection, found in this devotional guide.
- **As a family, talk through the discussion question together.** Close with the short prayer found at the bottom of the page.

Each reflection includes a simple craft or recipe suggestion to go with it. You could do this as part of the reflection, or at another time to remind you of some of the ideas you've been exploring.

What else is in this resource?

As well as all-age devotions, you'll find a little 'big' thought that draws on the same themes but is aimed specifically at adults. Each one includes suggestions for further reflection and a short prayer. This could be something you reflect on while your child engages in the craft, or you might choose to read it over a cup of tea, by yourself, later on.

At **Little Worship Company**, we want to provide you with practical ideas for making your faith part of family life. In this book, you'll find some of our top tips on reading the Bible (page 23), as well as some of our favourite psalms for different life seasons (page 37).

Old or young, big or small – every single one of us is precious to God!

You'll probably spot a few LOVE BUGS on our pages. They might be little – but they remind us of God's BIG love for us.

So do I, Hal. And God loves it when we praise Him too!
I love parties - and I love praise parties the best! I love singing and dancing and jumping to God!
Praise parties ARE fun. But there are lots of ways to prais God. We can use every part of us to thank God and to show Him how much we love Him. Let's find out how together!

Praise Party

Devotion 1	Praise God with happy songs	**10**
Devotion 2	Praise God with your soul and strength	**14**
Devotion 3	Praise God with loud instruments	**18**
	Praise in the Psalms	**23**
Devotion 4	Praise God with following footsteps	**24**
Devotion 5	Praise God with thankful hearts	**28**
Devotion 6	Praise God with helpful hands	**32**
	A psalm for all seasons	**37**
Devotion 7	Praise God with all my friends	**38**
Devotion 8	Praise God with everything I've got	**42**
	Crafts and recipes	**46**
	Praise Party **thank you prayers**	**48**

1 Praise God with happy songs

Think about the best news you ever heard. How does it make you feel? What does it make you do? It's hard to stay quiet. You want to cheer and sing as loudly as you can. And you can't keep still. Happy news makes us want to clap our hands and jump around!

The best news of all is that God made us, loves us and is always with us. That's why the Bible is packed full of people praising God. When they see how brilliant He is, they burst into song! And people are still singing today. All over the world, people are praising God for His amazing love. God loves to hear our praises. **So let's all sing and cheer and jump and dance to God!**

We praise God because He's amazing! Talk about all the things God has done for you and your family. What words describe God? Say thank you to Him!

We can join with Christians all over the world in praising God. Ask a grown-up to make a 'heart' stamp out of a potato or something similar. Draw a picture of yourself and the place where you live. Stamp hearts all over your picture, to remind yourself that God loves you and that we can love Him too.

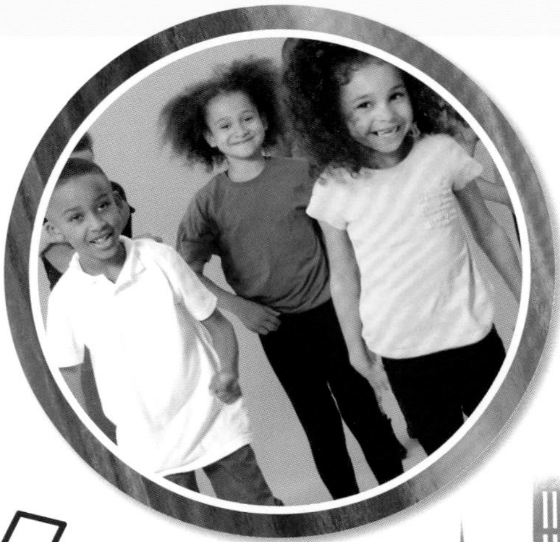

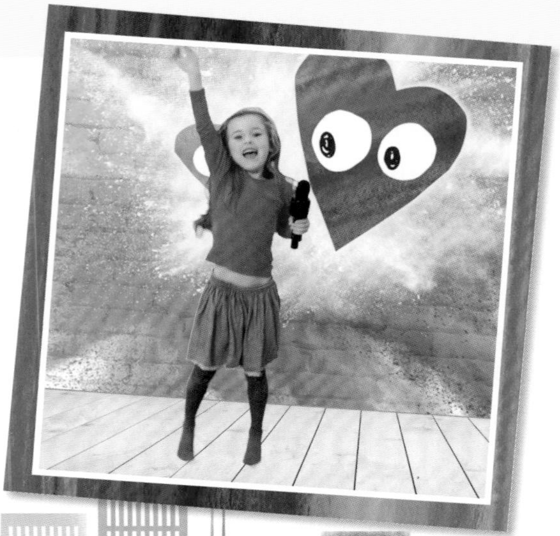

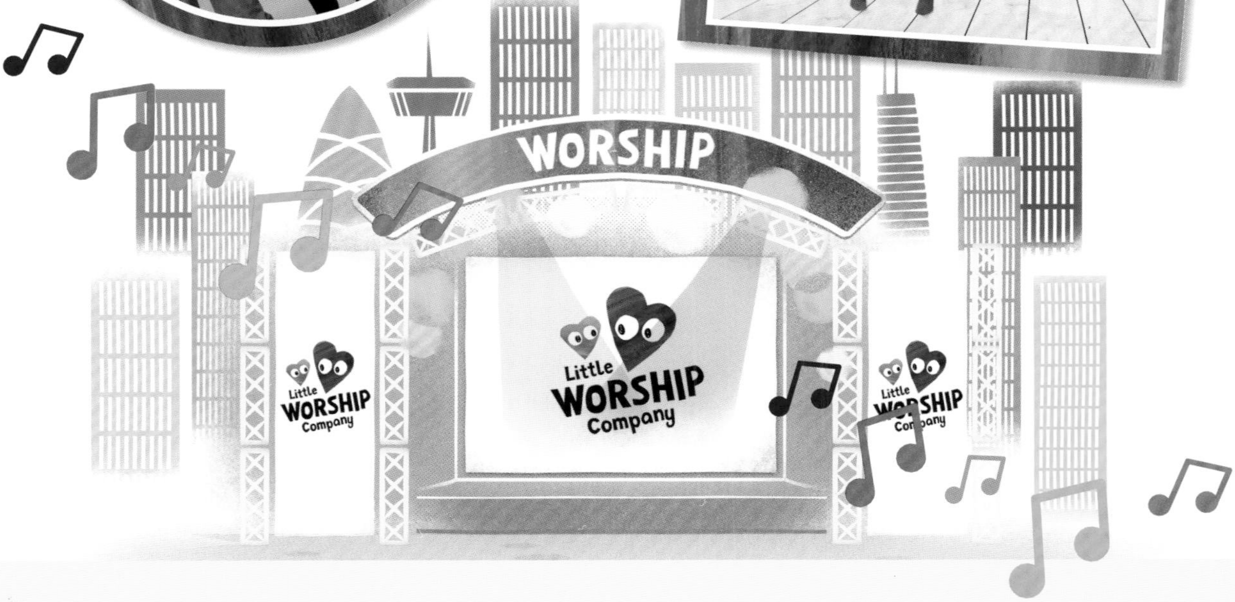

Dear God, **thank you for my loud voice to sing to You.** Thank you for my bouncy legs to dance to You. Thank you that You are so amazing, so kind and so loving. **Amen.**

1 TIME TO REFLECT

Psalm 96

Sing to the Lord a new song; sing to the Lord, all the earth.
Sing to the Lord, praise his name; proclaim his salvation day after day.
Declare his glory among the nations, his marvelous deeds among all peoples.
For great is the Lord and most worthy of praise; he is to be feared above all gods.
For all the gods of the nations are idols, but the Lord made the heavens.
Splendour and majesty are before him; strength and glory are in his sanctuary.
Ascribe to the Lord, all you families of nations, ascribe to the Lord glory and strength.
Ascribe to the Lord the glory due his name; bring an offering and come into his courts.
Worship the Lord in the splendor of his holiness; tremble before him, all the earth.
Say among the nations, "The Lord reigns."
The world is firmly established, it cannot be moved; he will judge the peoples with equity.
Let the heavens rejoice, let the earth be glad; let the sea resound, and all that is in it.
Let the fields be jubilant, and everything in them; let all the trees of the forest sing for joy.
Let all creation rejoice before the Lord, for he comes, he comes to judge the earth.
He will judge the world in righteousness and the peoples in his faithfulness.

Praise is the soundtrack to Scripture. In the Old Testament, God's people sing epic songs of praise to celebrate God's victory and might. Songs burst from the pages of Israel's great hymn book, the Psalms. Praise flows from individual men and women of faith after life-changing encounters with God – as in Hannah's prayer after God grants her a child (1 Samuel 2), or Mary's song in Luke 1. Doxologies, hymns sung by the early Christians, are scattered throughout Paul's letters to the early church. Some of the simplest and most memorable exclamations of praise are those said by the angels, such as the one the shepherds heard (Luke 2) or those said at the throne of God Himself (Revelation 4).

Why does praise feature so heavily in the Bible? Ultimately, because God deserves it. As the psalmist writes, ***"Great is the Lord and most worthy of praise"*** (verse 4).

AND AS WE SEEK TO FOLLOW GOD, PRAISE SHOULD BE A KEY FEATURE IN OUR LIVES TOO.

It's part and parcel of knowing Him. The more we see of God, His majesty and His goodness, the more we want to praise Him. But praise also gets the dynamic of our relationship right. We live in a highly 'individualistic' culture – one that puts 'me' and 'my needs' first. But when we come to God in praise, we put ourselves, our desires and even our concerns to one side, to give God that which is His due. We lay down who we are to declare all that God is – and to celebrate all that God has done and continues to do, in the world and in our lives.

TIME TO ACT

1 Praising God includes telling Him how great He is, thanking Him for all He has done and expressing our love for Him. Take some time now to sing or speak praise to God. You might want to use a psalm from the Bible, such as Psalm 96, or you could use more modern worship songs.

2 In 1 Chronicles 16, where Psalm 96 is originally found, David calls the Levites to lead the people into praise. Sometimes, we need to be the ones to lead our family into a place of thanksgiving and praise. Think about ways you might make praise and thanksgiving common features of your day-to-day family life.

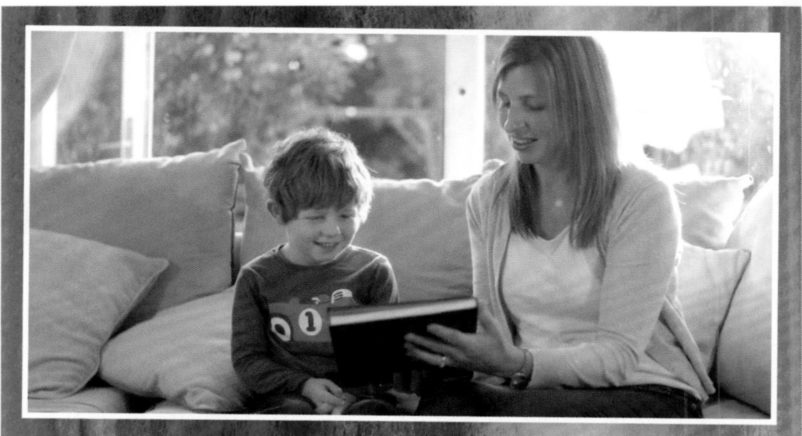

TIME TO PRAY

I praise You, God, for all that You are –
my Maker, Provider, Healer and Saviour.

I praise You, God, for all that You have done and all that You continue to do.

May You find a song of praise on my lips,
now and always.

Amen.

BIG

ONLY GOT A MINUTE?

- Encounters with God lead to praise.
- Praising God changes the dynamic of our relationship with Him.
- When we come to God in praise, we put ourselves, our desires and our concerns to one side.
- Choosing to praise God recentres us, allowing us to truly celebrate all that He has done and continues to do, in the world and in our lives.
- How might you make praise and thanksgiving important in your day-to-day family life?

2 Praise God with your soul and strength

Luke 10:27

Love the Lord your God with all your heart, with all your soul, with all your mind and with all your strength.

I feel like my heart is full of love for God!

That's great, Hal! The more you love God, the more you want to praise Him and make Him happy.

Can you find your hand? What about your foot? Your nose? Your knees? Well done! Can you find your heart? What about your mind? Your soul? It's not so easy to find these. But they are very important. They're the bits inside of us which choose what we think, say and do. And we can praise God with them too!

Loving God with heart, soul, mind and strength means making God the most important person in our lives. It means loving Him best, putting Him first, and giving Him our all. **It's not always easy to love somebody we can't see.** But we can get to know God and the things He loves by reading about Him in the Bible.

TALK TOGETHER

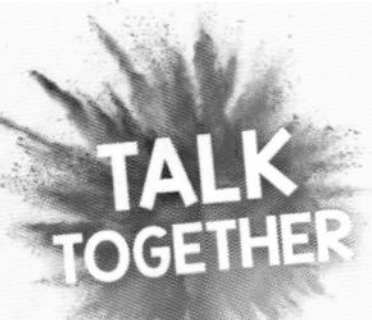

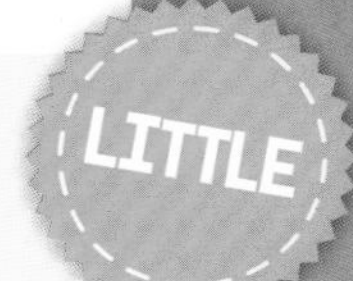

Talk about all the different ways you show people that you love them. How can you show God that you love Him? **What makes God happy?**

MAKE TOGETHER

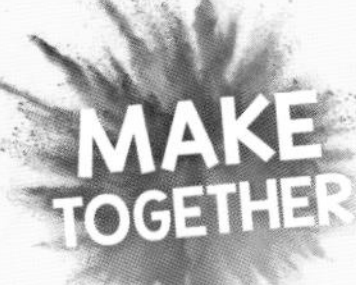

We can love God with every part of our body. We can praise him with our breath. Make some paper windmills, which turn when you blow hard. You can't see the wind that pushes them but you can see the result. Just like the wind, we can't see God, but we can see the marvellous things he has done.

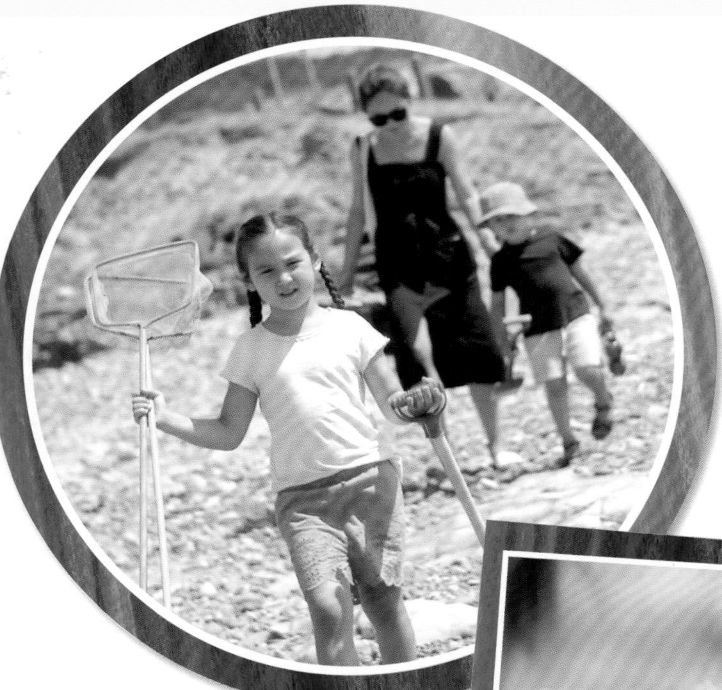

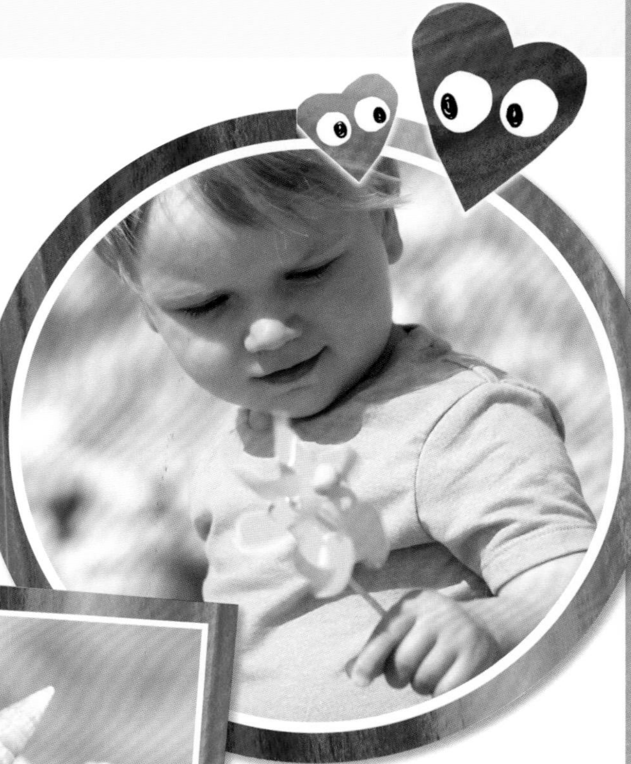

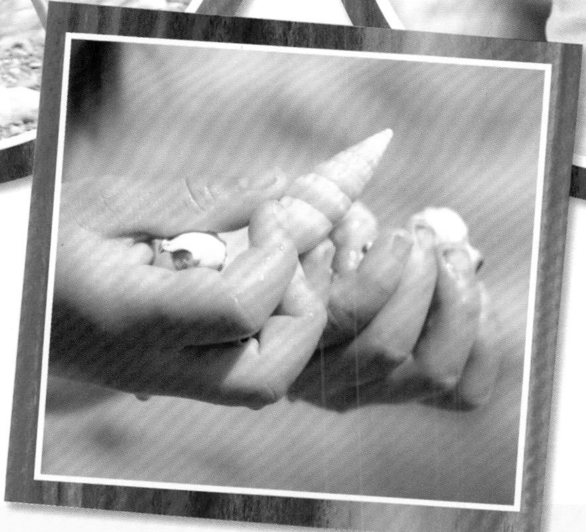

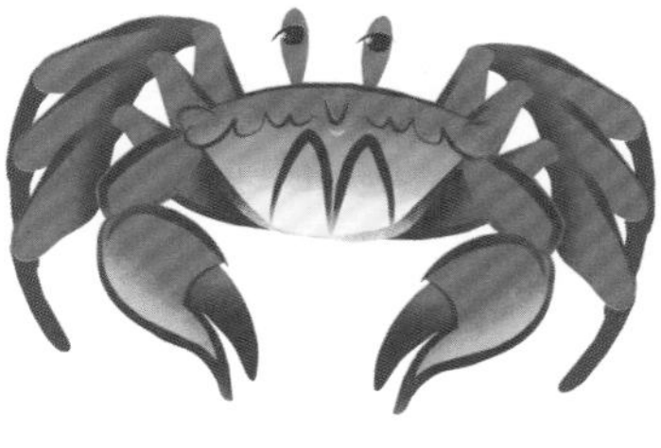

PRAY TOGETHER

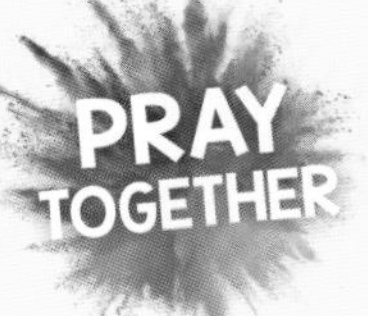

Dear God, **thank you that You love me more than I can imagine.** Help me to love You too, with every part of me. **Amen.**

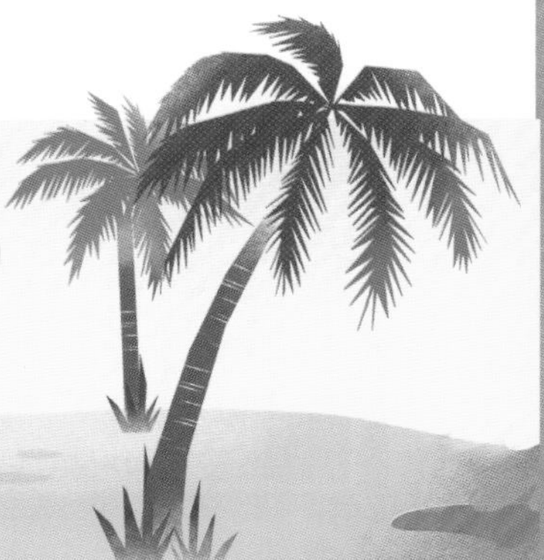

2 TIME TO REFLECT

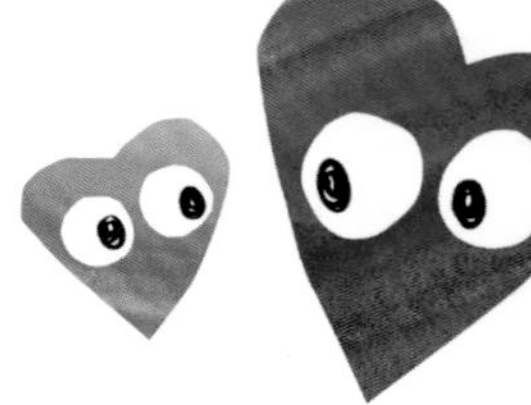

Luke 10:25-28

On one occasion an expert in the law stood up to test Jesus. "Teacher," he asked, "what must I do to inherit eternal life?"

"What is written in the Law?" he replied. "How do you read it?"

He answered, "'Love the Lord your God with all your heart and with all your soul and with all your strength and with all your mind'; and, 'Love your neighbour as yourself.'"

"You have answered correctly," Jesus replied. "Do this and you will live."

It's often said that we only see the tip of an iceberg. Dive underneath the surface and you'll discover a whole mountain of ice below. The same is true of our praise. What we say or sing isn't the sum of our praise. Rather, it's an outward expression of something bigger and deeper within us: our love for God.

TRUE PRAISE BEGINS IN THE HEART.

It flows from a commitment to the ancient command, reiterated by Jesus Himself, to love God with all our heart, soul, mind and strength. The Bible asks us to orientate every part of our lives towards God – our words, actions, thoughts and dreams – all for Him and His glory. Anything less is merely paying lip-service to Him.

Real worship, then, involves giving every part of ourselves to God. And yet, far from losing out, we find we're left with more than we started with. When Jesus says, ***"Do this and you will live"***, he isn't talking about gaining brownie points with God or earning a ticket into heaven. There's a sense here that giving our all to God is what makes us really come alive. Again, this command – to love God and love our neighbour as ourselves – is at odds with modern Western culture. It places 'me', my dreams and my desires some way down the pecking order. But the Bible promises that the more we give, the more we will receive (Luke 6:38). When we place all that we are and all that we have in God's hands, we discover that God will do more in us and through us than we could ever ask or imagine.

TIME TO ACT

1 Take some time to reflect on what it means to love God with heart, soul, mind and strength. You might like to ask yourself:

- **Heart:** What or who is your number one priority?
- **Soul:** What do you strive after? What are you ambitious for?
- **Mind:** What or whom do you spend most of your time thinking about?
- **Strength:** What do you use most of your time, money and energy for?

2 Read Deuteronomy 6:4-9, where this teaching first appears. It instructs parents to impress God's commands on their children and embed them into family life. How might you learn to love God and follow His commands as a family? Can you think of any opportunities to serve God together?

TIME TO PRAY

Thank you, Father, that You love me.

I'm sorry for the times when I fail to love You as I should.

Help me to give You the very best of me – heart, soul, mind and strength.

Amen.

60 SECONDS

ONLY GOT A MINUTE?

- True praise flows from a commitment to love God, with all our heart, soul, mind and strength.
- Real worship involves giving every part of us to God.
- When we place all that we are and all that we have in God's hands, we discover that He will do more in us, and through us, than we could ever ask or imagine.
- What do you strive after? What are you ambitious for? What are God's ambitions for you?

Praise God with loud instruments

Based on Psalm 150:3-5 (LWC)

Praise God – He is so great! Praise Him with the loud trumpet. Praise Him with guitars and violins. Praise Him with drums and whistles. Praise Him with tambourines and maracas!

Do you have any musical instruments? There are so many to choose from! Some you hit – like big loud drums. Some you shake – like jingling bells and tambourines. Some you blow – like trumpets, recorders and kazoos. Some you strum – like guitars. And on a keyboard, you let your fingers go for a LONG run!

We can use all of these to praise God. People have been making music to God for thousands of years. In Bible times, people used horns, cymbals and harps to make big, beautiful sounds to God. Sometimes music can show our feelings better that words can. We might not know how to tell God we love Him. **But we can make a happy noise to Him to show Him!**

TALK TOGETHER

How many instruments can you name? What sounds do they make? Which do you like best? Think about how God loves to hear praise music – because He loves the people who play it to Him!

MAKE TOGETHER

We can praise God by making music to Him. Why don't you have a go at making your own instruments? Try filling empty jam jars with different amounts of water and then tap them with a metal teaspoon. Lots of water makes low deep notes and a little water makes high notes. You can also bang big saucepans with a wooden spoon to make a drum, or make shakers by filling empty plastic bottles with a handful of dried rice or pasta. Make sure you screw the lid on tight!

PRAY TOGETHER

Dear God, **thank you for beautiful music.** Thank you for all the different sounds I can make for You. Help me to praise You wherever I am and whatever I'm doing. **Amen.**

3 TIME TO REFLECT

Psalm 150

Praise the Lord.

Praise God in his sanctuary; praise him in his mighty heavens.

Praise him for his acts of power; praise him for his surpassing greatness.

Praise him with the sounding of the trumpet, praise him with the harp and lyre,
praise him with tambourine and dancing, praise him with the strings and pipe,
praise him with the clash of cymbals, praise him with resounding cymbals.

Let everything that has breath praise the Lord.

Praise the Lord.

The Book of Psalms is arguably the finest worship book in history. And this final psalm is one last rallying cry to praise God. In many ways it sums up the whole subject – a kind of 'blueprint' for community praise. In just six verses, it outlines where we should praise (verse 1), why we should praise (verse 2), how we should praise (verses 3-5) and who is invited to praise God (verse 6). To anybody used to going to church regularly, this will all look and sound familiar. The psalmist calls people to the 'sanctuary' – that is, somewhere holy and set apart, for praise purposes – where they're called to make music, sing and dance in celebration of all that God is and all that He's done.

But this psalm does more than just offer a template for worship. It reminds us how wonderful it is to praise God together – that it is *good* to make a big noise in His honour. It sounds obvious, but it's something that, in our digital age, we can sometimes forget. The internet has given us a host of worship and teaching resources at our fingertips, as well as access to online faith forums. It would be very easy for praise to become something we offer quietly and privately. But there's a dynamic that comes from worshipping together that pleases God and increases our own faith. What's more, it provides an important witness within our communities.

GOD'S HEART IS THAT ALL COME TO KNOW AND PRAISE HIM.

Our worship points others towards the One that it's for. And the louder the praise, the more people will hear it.

TIME TO ACT

1 Psalm 150 says:

Praise him for his acts of power,
Praise him for his magnificent greatness.

Psalm 150:2 (The Message)

Say, write or draw what this means to you.

2 We sometimes think of our Christian life as a solo run. But it's more like a marathon event, with thousands of people running together and cheering each other on. Take some time to pray for your church family. Pray for the leaders as they seek to serve God and your community. Pray for all those who are involved in leading or supporting the children's ministry.

TIME TO PRAY

Thank you, God, that we can praise You.

Thank you that we are invited to be part of your big story for all of creation.

Help us to declare Your goodness loudly enough for all to hear.

Amen.

BIG

ONLY GOT A MINUTE?

- The Bible is full of stories of people joining together to worship God.
- Joining with others to worship together pleases God and increases our own faith.
- Sometimes we can think of our Christian life as a solo run. But it's more like a marathon event, with thousands of people running together and cheering each other on.
- Pray for your church family and for those who encourage you in your faith. How can you be an 'encourager' to those around you?

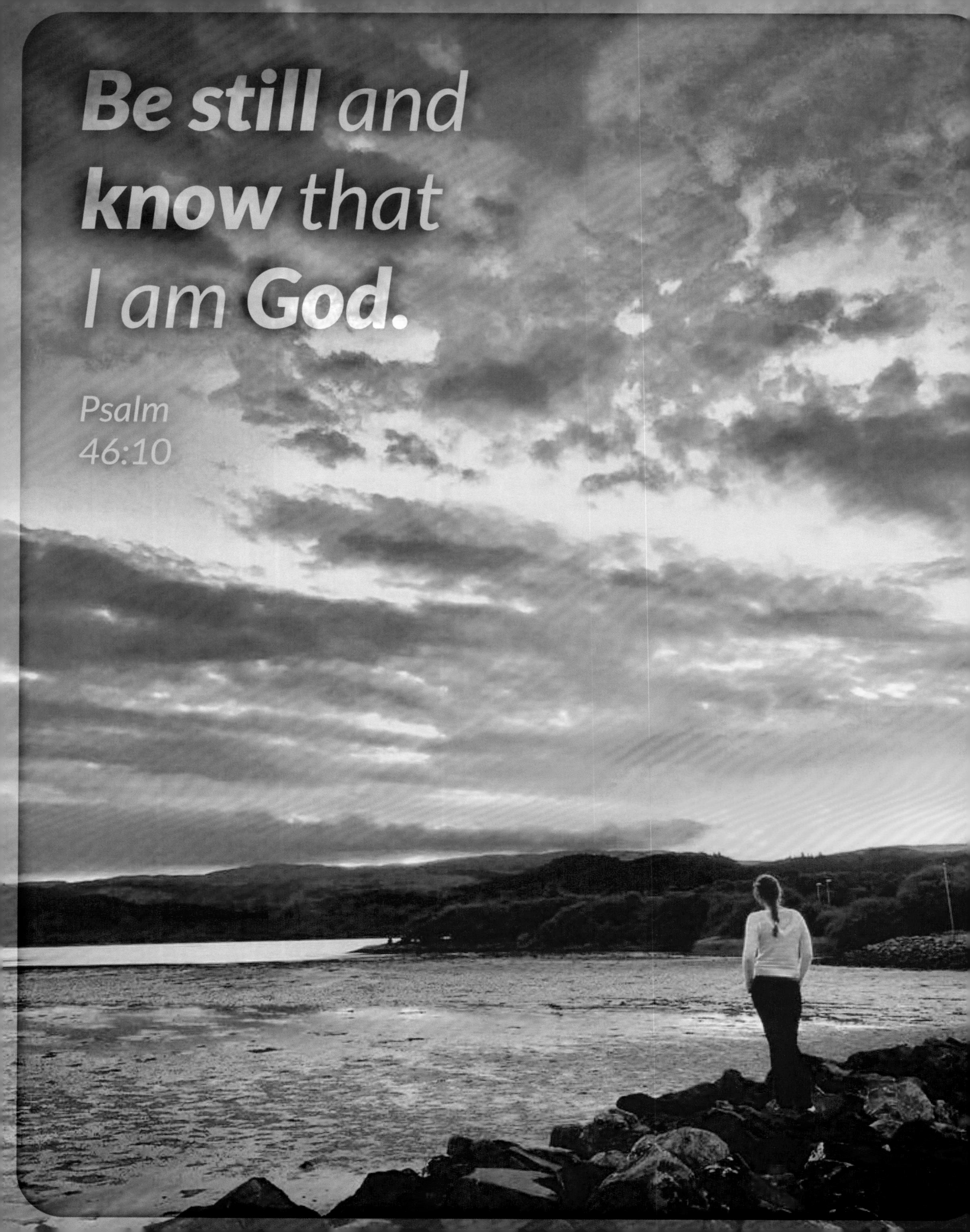

Be still *and*
know *that*
I am **God.**

Psalm
46:10

Praise in the Psalms

A TEN-MINUTE MEDITATION

You will need a quiet space, a Bible, a notebook and a pen.

- **Find a quiet space.** Sit down and make yourself comfortable. Breathe slowly and deeply. Become aware of God's presence with you and thank Him.
- **Choose a psalm to read** – for example, Psalm 23. Invite God's Spirit to speak to you as you read.
- **Slowly read through the psalm once.** Slowly read through the psalm again. Look back over the psalm. Was there a particular verse that stood out to you?
- **Meditate on the verse** by emphasising each word in turn. For example, verse 6:

    Surely *your goodness and love will follow me all the days of my life…*

    Surely ***your*** *goodness and love will follow me all the days of my life…*

    Surely your ***goodness*** *and love will follow me all the days of my life…*

- **What is God revealing to you** as you reflect on these words? How is He encouraging you? How is He challenging you?
- **Use these reflections** as you pray and praise.
- **If you have time…** Rewrite the psalm or a section of the psalm in your own words. Alternatively, draw a picture based on your reflections. Use it as a means of praising God.

4 Praise God with following footsteps

Have you got a best friend? What are they like? When we make friends, we get to know them. We find out what makes them happy and what they like to do. And we have *lots* of fun doing those things together!

It's a bit like this with God. One big reason to praise God is because He's our friend. And being friends with God means getting to know Him and learning to follow Him. We can do this by looking at Jesus. **The Bible says that God sent his Son, Jesus, to live with us.** We can see what's special to God – what He cares about – by seeing all that Jesus did. And nothing makes God happier than when we learn to do those things too.

TALK TOGETHER

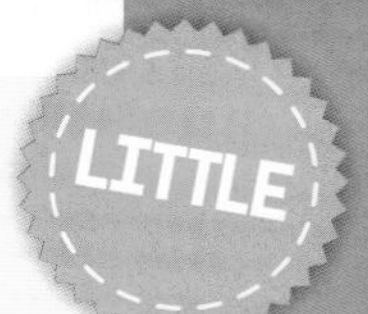

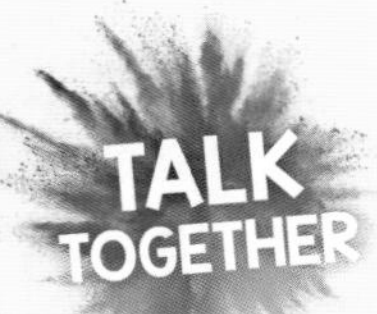

Look at the stories of Jesus in the gospels. What kinds of things did Jesus do? What does it say about what God is like – what He cares about? How can we do likewise?

MAKE TOGETHER

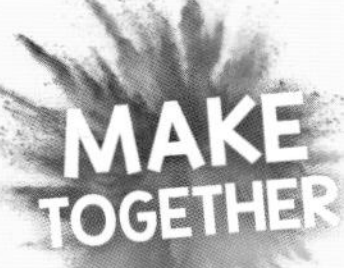

We can praise God by following in Jesus' footsteps. Do some feet-painting pictures… As you do them, think about how learning about Jesus and doing what He did makes God really happy!

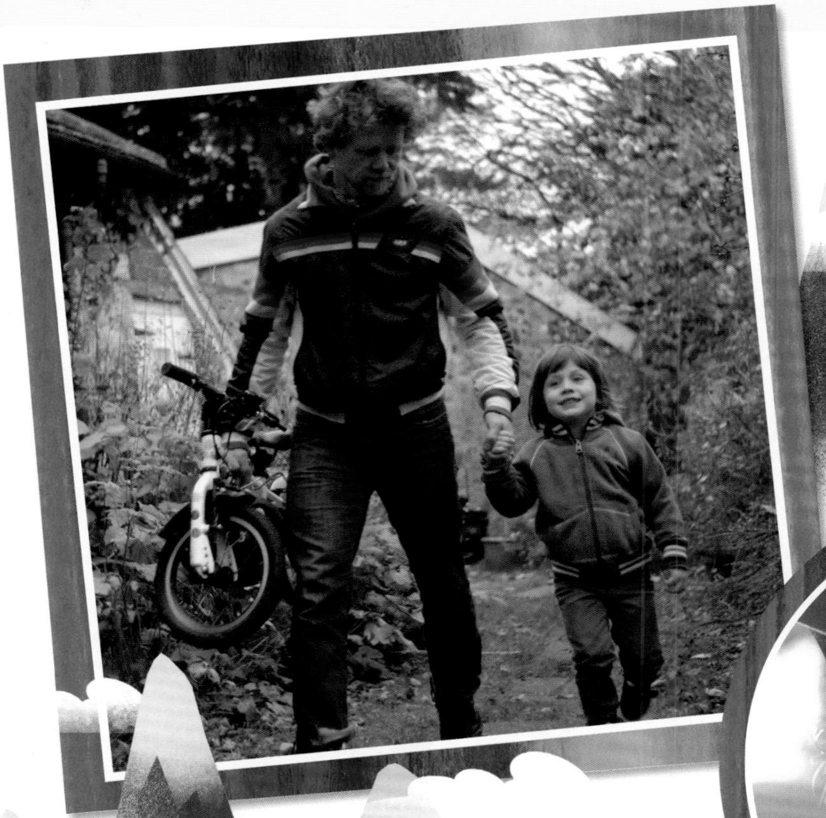

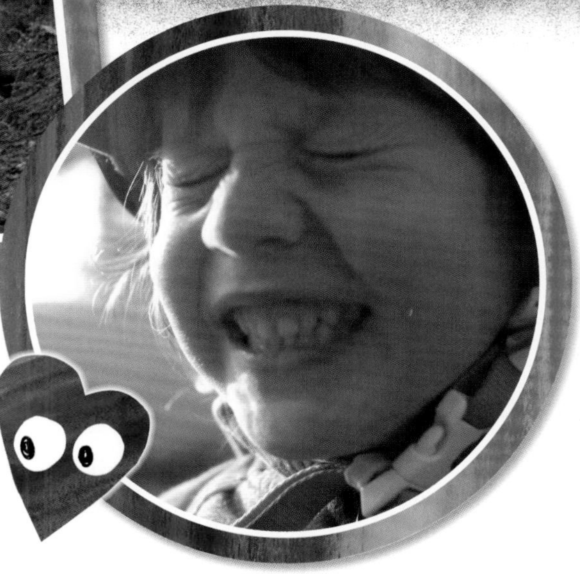

PRAY TOGETHER

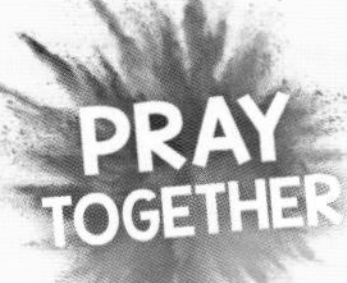

Dear God, **thank you that You are my best friend.** Thank you for sending Jesus to show me what You are like. Help me to follow in Your footsteps every day. **Amen.**

4 TIME TO REFLECT

Ephesians 5:1-2 (The Message)

Watch what God does, and then you do it, like children who learn proper behaviour from their parents. Mostly what God does is love you. Keep company with him and learn a life of love. Observe how Christ loved us. His love was not cautious but extravagant. He didn't love in order to get something from us but to give everything of himself to us. Love like that.

"Praise the LORD, my soul, and forget not all his benefits – who forgives all your sins and heals all your diseases..." (Psalm 103:2-3). God's goodness is a recurring theme throughout the Psalms. They paint a picture of a God who loves passionately and cares tenderly. And this portrait gains a new dimension in Jesus. For in Jesus, the invisible God became visible. "No one has ever seen God," John wrote, "but the one and only Son... has made him known" (John 1:18). Jesus lives all that the Psalms declare. He heals the sick. He welcomes the lonely. He lifts up the humble. He binds up the broken-hearted. The more we see of Jesus, the more we begin to grasp just how deep the Father's love runs. And our response is surely one of wonder and worship.

But this is only half the story. 'Watch what God does, and then you do it,' Paul tells the Ephesians. "Observe how Christ loved us... Love like that." It's God's desire that we become like Him, "walking in the way of love" (verse 2, NIV). But rather than give us a textbook, He gives us Jesus. As we spend time with Him, we see what matters to God. How His love is not just for 'me', but for my neighbour. And for the poor and marginalised – those at the edges of our communities. The more we're with Him, the more we'll become like Him – following in His footsteps and offering hope in all we say and do. In Jesus, God invites us to experience His immense love for us.

AS WE "KEEP COMPANY" WITH HIM, LET'S PRAY THAT IT'S NOT JUST OUR HEARTS THAT ARE MOVED IN PRAISE, BUT OUR FEET TOO.

TIME TO ACT

1 Paul writes that we should "keep company" with God. Jesus shows us the importance of finding rest and refreshment with the Father, regularly retreating from the hustle and bustle of a busy life to spend time with God. Find some time today to rest in God's presence – whether that's with music, the Bible or simply silence. You might like to try our ten-minute meditation, found on **page 23**.

2 As we look at Jesus, we don't just discover how God loves us, but how we are to love in turn. Who would Jesus be spending time with in your community and friendship circle? Where might God be calling you to follow Him? Pray for God's strength to go where He's leading you.

TIME TO PRAY

Thank you, God,
that we love because You first loved us.

Help me to see more of You.

Help me to be more like You.

Lead me in a life of love,
walking with You each step of the way.

Amen.

ONLY GOT A MINUTE?

- The Psalms describe a God who loves us passionately and cares for us tenderly.
- In Jesus, this invisible God becomes visible.
- The more we see of Jesus, the more we begin to grasp how much God loves us.
- Through Jesus, God invites us to experience His immense love for us. As we ***"keep company"*** with Him, let not just our hearts be moved in praise, but our feet too, as we share His love with those around us.
- Find a moment to ***"keep company"*** with God today.

5 Praise God with thankful hearts

Some words are really special. And there are two words that make people really happy when we say them. We might say them after we get a present. Or when somebody gives us a tasty meal. Or when someone helps us with something that's a bit tricky. Do you know what they are? That's right – THANK YOU!

The Bible says that we can praise God by saying "thank you" to Him. He has done so much for us. He made a wonderful world that we can enjoy. He gives us all we need, like clothes and food and family. And best of all, He gave us Jesus. Because of Jesus, we can be friends with God forever. **And that's worth the biggest THANK YOU of them all!**

TALK TOGETHER

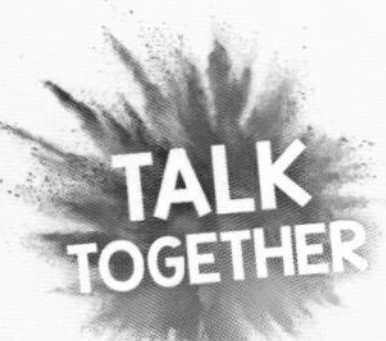

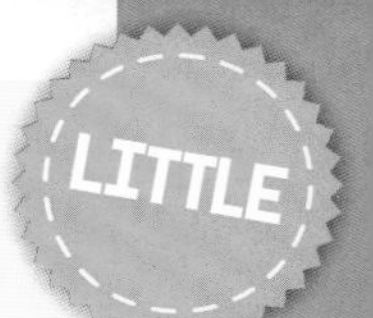

There's so much to thank God for! Can you think of five things to say thank you for today? You might want to draw them on sticky notes and put them up around the house, so you never forget to thank God!

MAKE TOGETHER

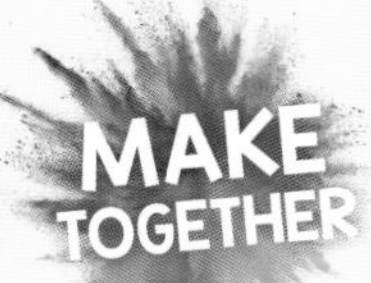

Nothing will ever stop us from being God's friend. Create a 'thankfulness peacock' using a paper plate, coloured card and paint. Cut a skittle-shaped head and body out of the coloured card and stick it onto the plate. Draw or stick two eyes and a beak onto the card. Make incisions in the paper plate towards the body to create feathers. On each feather, write something to be thankful for. Decorate your peacock with paint and glitter.

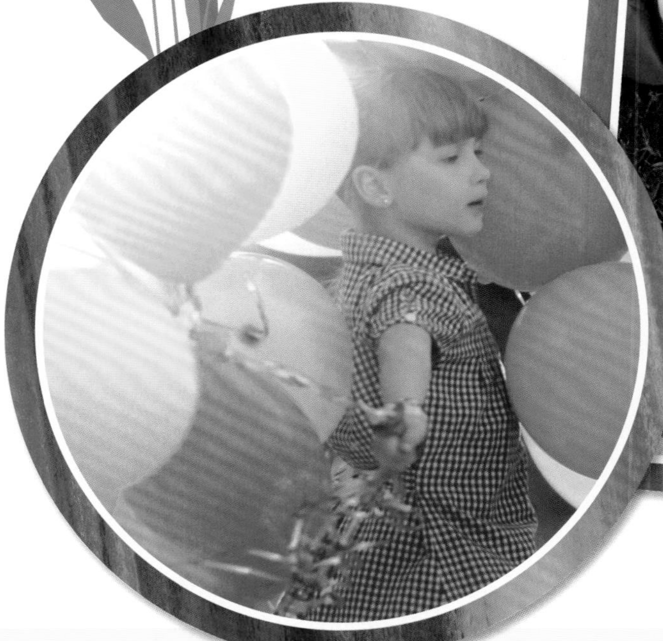

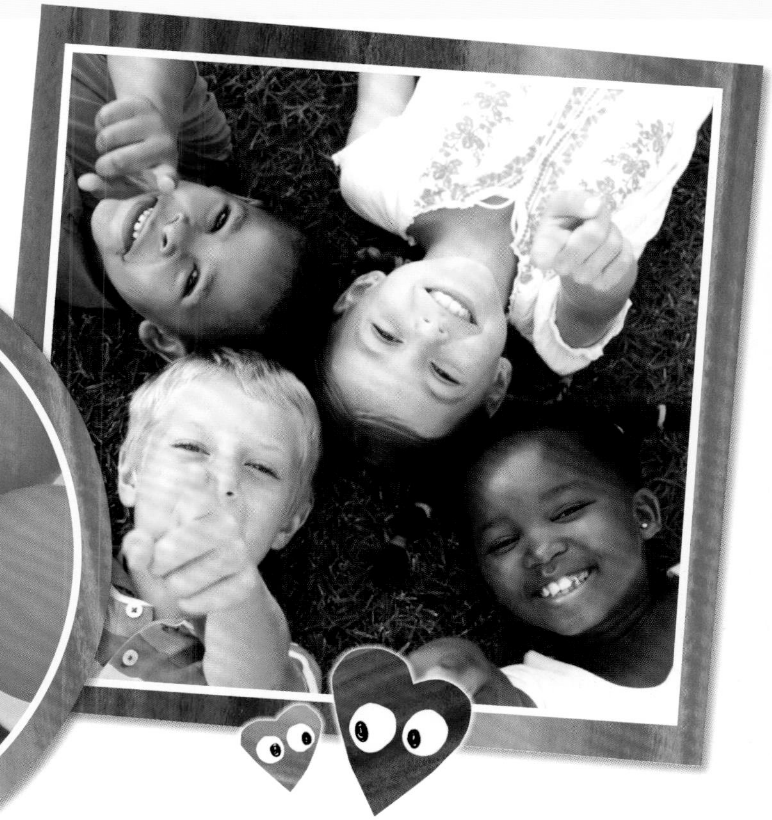

PRAY TOGETHER

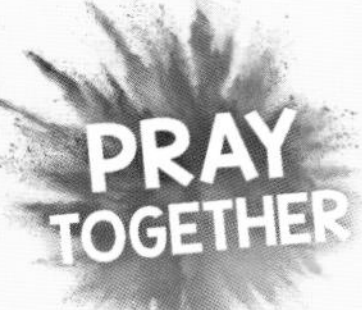

Dear God, **thank you for all that You give to me.** Thank you for food and clothes, for friends and family. Thank you that You sent Jesus so that I can always be Your friend. **Amen.**

5 TIME TO REFLECT

Psalm 136

Give thanks to the Lord, for he is good. His love endures for ever.
Give thanks to the God of gods. His love endures for ever.
Give thanks to the Lord of lords: His love endures for ever.
to him who alone does great wonders, His love endures for ever.
who by his understanding made the heavens, His love endures for ever.
who spread out the earth upon the waters, His love endures for ever.
who made the great lights – His love endures for ever.
the sun to govern the day, His love endures for ever.
the moon and stars to govern the night; His love endures for ever.
to him who struck down the firstborn of Egypt His love endures for ever.
and brought Israel out from among them His love endures for ever.
with a mighty hand and outstretched arm; His love endures for ever.
to him who divided the Red Sea asunder His love endures for ever.
and brought Israel through the midst of it, His love endures for ever.
but swept Pharaoh and his army into the Red Sea; His love endures for ever.
to him who led his people through the wilderness; His love endures for ever.
to him who struck down great kings, His love endures for ever.
and killed mighty kings – His love endures for ever.
Sihon king of the Amorites His love endures for ever.
and Og king of Bashan – His love endures for ever.
and gave their land as an inheritance, His love endures for ever.
an inheritance to his servant Israel. His love endures for ever.
He remembered us in our low estate His love endures for ever.
and freed us from our enemies. His love endures for ever.
He gives food to every creature. His love endures for ever.
Give thanks to the God of heaven. His love endures for ever.

Thanksgiving and praise are two sides of the same coin – so much so that if you look in the dictionary, you'll find 'praise' defined as 'expressing gratitude'. In Old Testament times, songs of praise were sung whilst thank-offerings were made in the temple – the two together a fitting celebration of God's victory and rescue. It's likely that Psalm 136 was used in this way. In this psalm, the leader calls on the congregation to thank God for all the marvellous things He has done. And there is so much to celebrate. God is not only an awesome Creator and Provider. He is also their wonderful Saviour. He freed them from slavery in Egypt and gave them an amazing inheritance – the

Promised Land. This is their story; this is their song – the reason for a thousand thanksgivings.

AND THIS IS OUR SONG TOO. GOD, OUR CREATOR AND PROVIDER, IS ALSO OUR SAVIOUR.

In Jesus, we have been rescued. We've been set free from the power of sin: now there's nothing to keep us from God's love. And we've been given a new inheritance. God calls us His children: we can know His presence, peace and power, today and forever more. This isn't just a nice theological idea. It's a story that changes our present reality and our future hope. Having been given such an incredible gift, saying thank you is just the beginning. In temple worship, praise was accompanied by an offering. As we celebrate all that God has done for us, we, too, are called to make an offering... in the words of the old hymn, nothing less than ***"my soul, my life, my all"*** (Isaac Watts).

TIME TO ACT

1 Write your own version of Psalm 136. List all the things God has done for you – the times when He has shown His love and faithfulness in your life. Add the refrain ***"His love endures forever"*** after each line.

2 We don't always find time to say thank you. We may need some help to make a habit of gratitude. Why not try setting an alarm on your phone for every couple of hours? When it pings, think of five things to thank God for – and thank Him!

TIME TO PRAY

Father God – You have given everything *to* me. You have given everything *for* me. Accept my thanks. Accept my praise. Accept my life, laid down to live for You.

Amen.

BIG

ONLY GOT A MINUTE?

- Psalm 136 reminds the congregation of God's enduring love, throughout their history.
- God intervened again and again to change their present reality and to give them a future hope.
- That same God is also our Saviour.
- In Jesus, we have been rescued. We've been set free from the power of sin, so now there's nothing to keep us from God's love.
- How can you create a habit of gratitude? Try setting an alarm on your phone each day. When it pings, think of five things to thank God for – and thank Him!

6 Praise God with helpful hands

Romans 12:10-13 (LWC)

Always love one another. Be joyful and faithful and patient. Share with people in need. Practise being kind.

There are lots of ways to let people know you love them. Telling them is one way. But we can show them too. Doing kind and helpful things shows people how much we care for them and it makes them happy.

It's the same with praising God. We can praise Him with songs and prayers. But we can also show Him how much we love Him by the things we do. In the Bible, God asks us to share His love with the people around us. Every time we help people in need, we make God happy. Every time we do kind things for others, we make God happy. And when we do all these things, **we show other people how much God loves them too!**

TALK TOGETHER

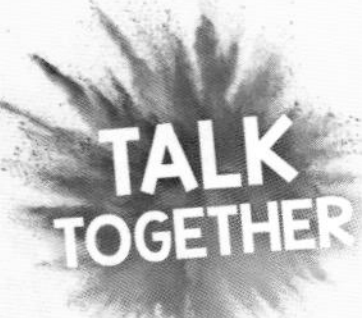

Think about how you could show God's love to those around you this week. What kind things could you do for the people in your street? Are there any people in your community who might need your help?

MAKE TOGETHER

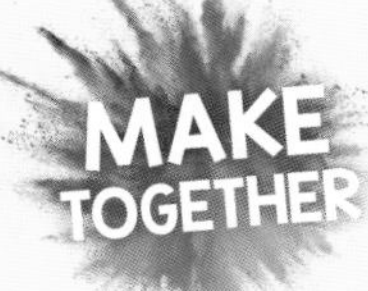

We can praise God by loving other people. Bake some 'love bug' biscuits. Why not share them with your friends and neighbours?

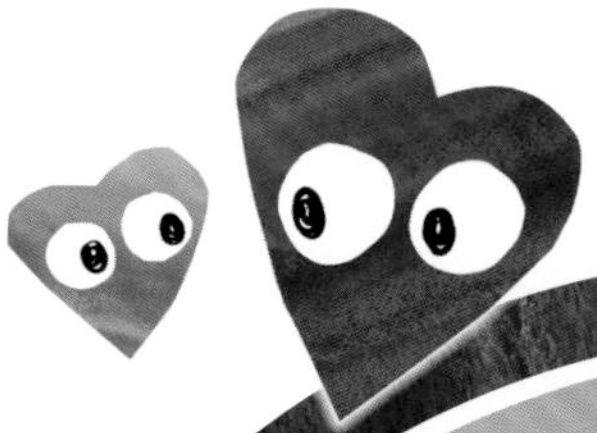

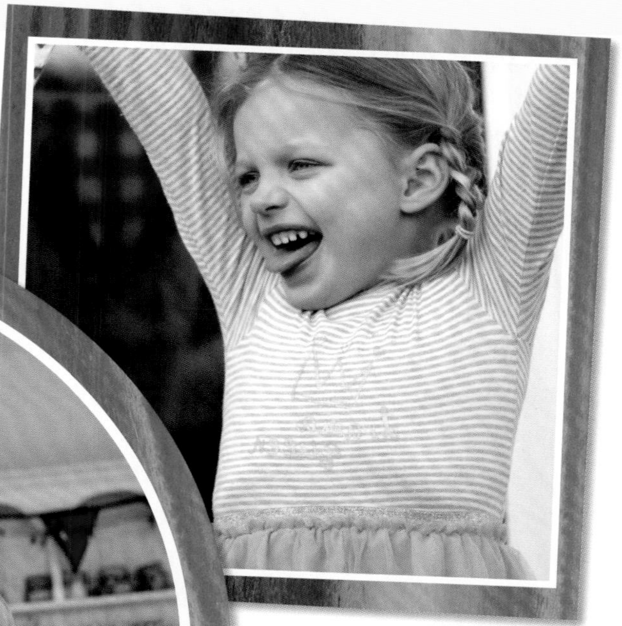

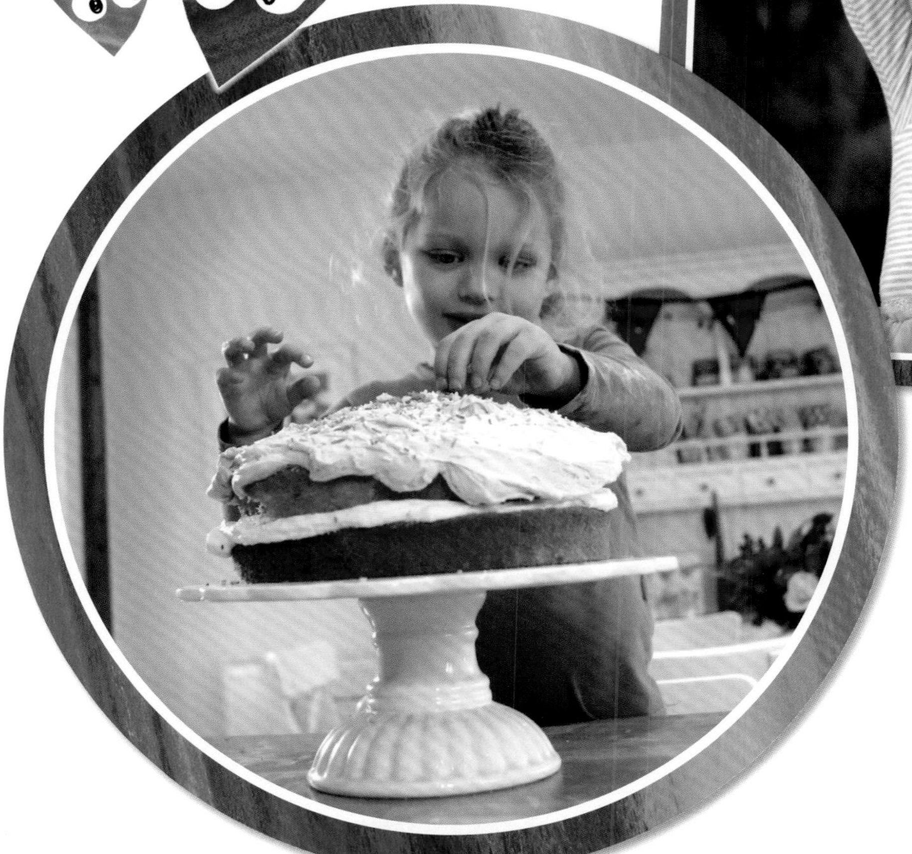

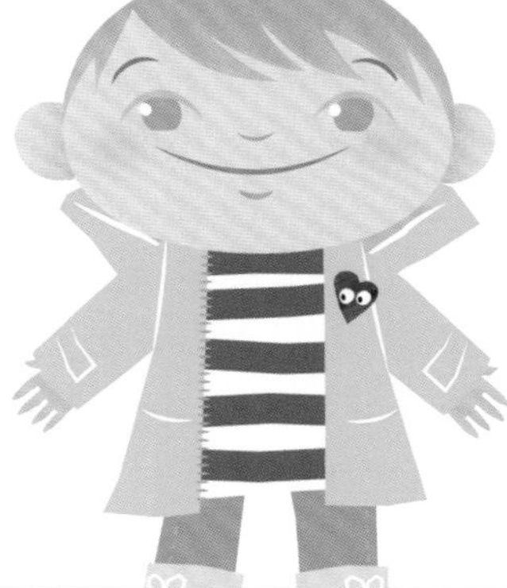

PRAY TOGETHER

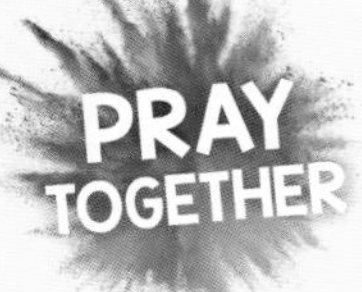

Dear God, **thank you that Your love for me is really BIG!** Help me to share Your love with other people so that they can see how much You love them too. **Amen.**

6 TIME TO REFLECT

Romans 12:9-18

Love must be sincere. Hate what is evil; cling to what is good. Be devoted to one another in love. Honour one another above yourselves. Never be lacking in zeal, but keep your spiritual fervour, serving the Lord. Be joyful in hope, patient in affliction, faithful in prayer. Share with the Lord's people who are in need. Practise hospitality.

Bless those who persecute you; bless and do not curse. Rejoice with those who rejoice; mourn with those who mourn. Live in harmony with one another. Do not be proud, but be willing to associate with people of low position. Do not be conceited.

Do not repay anyone evil for evil. Be careful to do what is right in the eyes of everyone. If it is possible, as far as it depends on you, live at peace with everyone.

When we think about 'praising God', it's probably the things we say or sing which spring to mind. But praise is also expressed in the things we do. Word and deed go hand in hand, because the things we do make good on the things we say. It's a connection that Jesus Himself makes to His disciples at the Last Supper: ***"If you love me,"*** He tells them, ***"keep my commands."*** (John 14:15). Praise is not just a matter of our mouths, then, but of our hearts and hands too. We can tell God how wonderful He is. We can acknowledge all He has done. We can really and truly feel the deepest gratitude for everything He has given to us. But the next step is to take our love for God and channel it into love for our neighbour.

Paul's words to the Romans show us what this looks like in practice.

AS CHRISTIANS, OUR LIVES ARE TO BE CHARACTERISED BY HUMILITY, GENEROSITY, SERVICE AND SACRIFICE.

We're called to be pastors (guiding and supporting others) and peacemakers. These are undoubtedly challenging commands to take on board. We naturally strive to do the best for our family. But what about our neighbours or our children's friends? Can we love them as we love ourselves? Paul asks that we practise hospitality. Are we willing to see our homes as God-given resources at His disposal? Are we prepared to disrupt our precious family traditions to show God's love to those who really need to see it? True obedience is hard – but God is worth it. As we learn to praise Him, may we always pray that our actions speak even louder than our words.

TIME TO ACT

1 Generosity flows from a thankful heart. Make a list of all the material resources you have. Pray over them with thanksgiving. How might God be asking you to use them – with your family and friends, your community, or further afield?

2 The Book of Amos underscores the importance of connecting words and deeds in our worship. In it, the people of God come under serious criticism for saying all the right things to God in the temple, whilst exploiting the poor in their day-to-day lives. In Amos 5:21-24, God emphatically rejects their songs and sacrifices, calling for justice and righteousness instead.

Amos reminds us again that love for God is expressed in love for neighbour – especially the vulnerable and oppressed. Spend some time researching organisations that are working to help those in crisis – for example, anti-slavery groups or homeless charities. How might you partner with them, in prayer or financially?

TIME TO PRAY

Father God – help me to love those around me, when it's easy and when it's difficult.

Please accept everything I am
and everything I have as an offering of praise.

Amen.

ONLY GOT A MINUTE?

- Praise isn't just expressed through our mouths; praise is also expressed in the things we do.
- An overflowing of praise results in an outpouring of love for those around us – our family, our neighbours, our community and our world.
- Generosity flows from a thankful heart. Thank God for all the material resources you have. How might God be asking you to use them as an offering of praise and thanksgiving?
- Who is your neighbour?

For the LORD
is **good** and His love
endures forever;
His **faithfulness** continues
through **all generations.**
Psalm
100:5

A psalm for all seasons

PRAYING AND PRAISING THROUGH THE PSALMS

Psalm 100

When you feel joyful –
or need to remind yourself of God's goodness...

... Enter His gates with thanksgiving and His courts with praise;
give thanks to Him and praise His name.
For the LORD is good and His love endures forever;
His faithfulness continues through all generations.

Psalm 23

When you feel blessed – or need to know that God cares...

The LORD is my shepherd, I lack nothing.
He makes me lie down in green pastures,
He leads me beside quiet waters, He refreshes my soul...

Psalm 46

When you feel anxious or afraid...

God is our refuge and strength, an ever-present help in trouble.
Therefore we will not fear, though the earth give way
and the mountains fall into the heart of the sea...

Psalm 25

When you feel like quitting...

Guard my life and rescue me;
do not let me be put to shame, for I take refuge in you.
May integrity and uprightness protect me,
because my hope, LORD, is in you.

Psalm 8

When you feel amazed by God's love –
or need to be reminded of how precious you are to Him...

When I consider your heavens, the work of your fingers,
the moon and the stars, which you have set in place,
what is mankind that you are mindful of them,
human beings that you care for them?

7 Praise God with all my friends

Ecclesiastes 3 (LWC)

There is a time for everything. A time to play, a time to sleep, a time to read, a time to bounce, a time to eat and a time to party!

Is it time for the praise party yet?

Yes, Hal. Get yourself ready – it's time to party!

Have you ever been to a party? What was it for? What did you do there? A party is a celebration. 'Celebrate' means being happy and having fun because of something or someone really special. We don't have parties every day. But it's important that we have them, because some things are worth celebrating!

There are lots of ways to praise God. We can tell God that we love Him quietly, when we're by ourselves. But God loves it when we throw Him a praise party! When we go to church, we meet up with our friends and celebrate God's great big love together. And the party's not just for us to enjoy. We can invite everyone we know to come and praise God too!

TALK TOGETHER

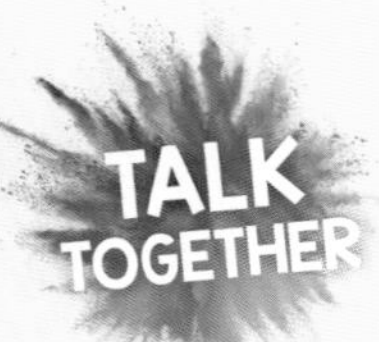

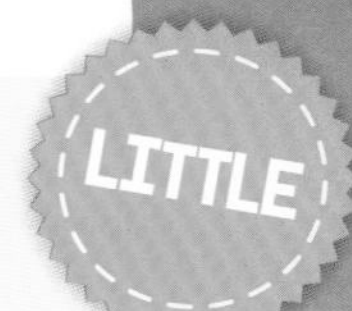

Talk about going to church. How is it like a party in God's honour? What other things do we do at church that make God happy? (For example: learning about Jesus.)

MAKE TOGETHER

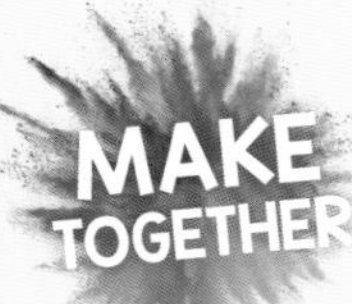

God's love for us deserves the biggest party in the world! Make paper chains out of strips of bright, coloured paper. Or stick coloured triangles to a long piece of string to make bunting. Write things to be thankful for on your paper chains/bunting. Put them up and have a praise party with your family and friends!

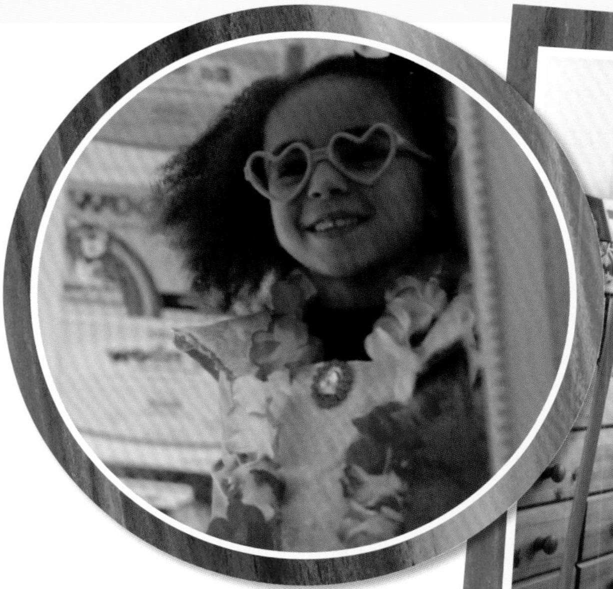

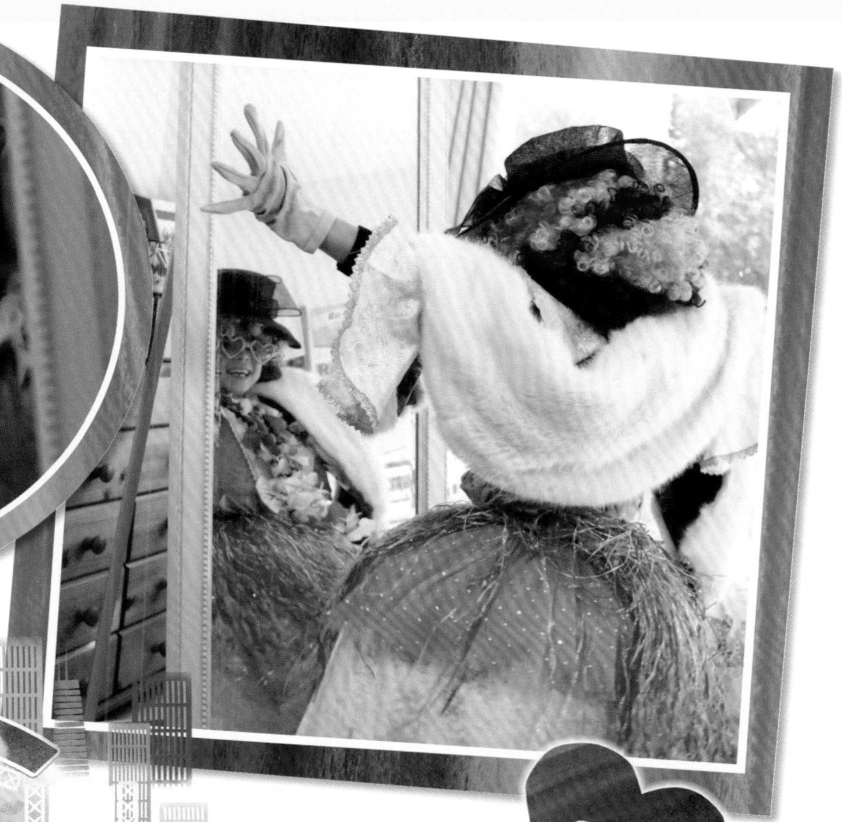

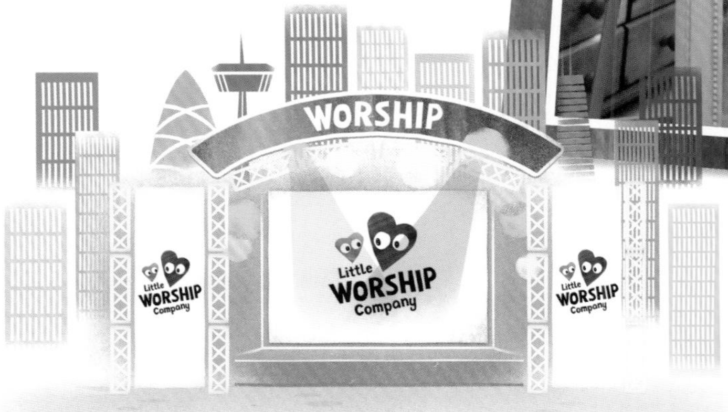

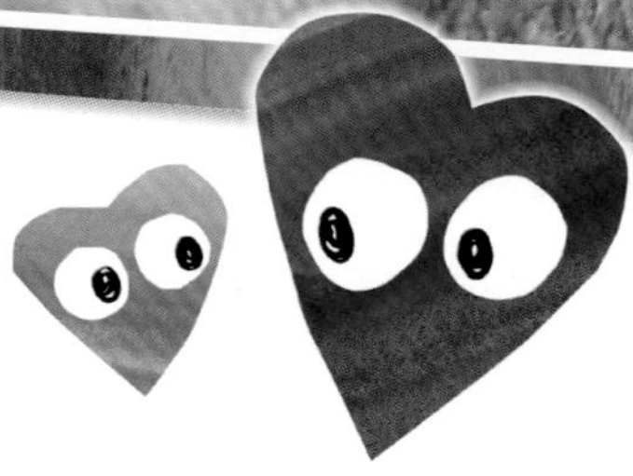

PRAY TOGETHER

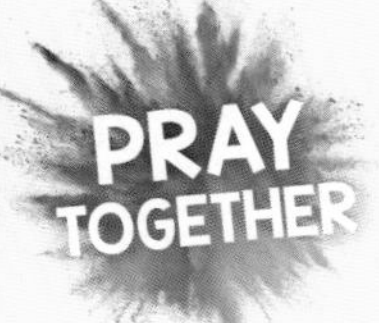

Dear God, **thank you for praise parties!** Thank you for special times to jump and sing to You with my friends. Thank you, too, that every day with You is special, because You are my friend. **Amen.**

7 TIME TO REFLECT

Ecclesiastes 3:1-8

There is a time for everything, and a season for every activity under the heavens:
a time to be born and a time to die, a time to plant and a time to uproot,
a time to kill and a time to heal, a time to tear down and a time to build,
a time to weep and a time to laugh, a time to mourn and a time to dance,
a time to scatter stones and a time to gather them, a time to embrace
and a time to refrain from embracing,
a time to search and a time to give up, a time to keep and a time to throw away,
a time to tear and a time to mend, a time to be silent and a time to speak,
a time to love and a time to hate, a time for war and a time for peace.

Some days it's easy to praise God. Other days it's really hard. Sometimes we feel God's presence and blessings. At other times, God feels distant, prayers seem to go unanswered and struggles seem to swamp us like a landslide. At these times, the last thing we might want to do is praise God. That's why it's helpful to read passages like the third chapter of Ecclesiastes. It reminds us that our lives will inevitably pass through different seasons. There'll be times when things are going well, when it's easy to praise and thank God. But there'll also be times of challenge or heartache, when it may take more emotional effort and commitment to praise God. At these times it can feel like a sacrifice.

This is one reason why being part of a worshipping church community is so helpful. It provides a spiritual rhythm to our lives, ensuring there's regular time set aside each week to praise God – however we may be feeling. It's worth noting that praise in the Bible is often referred to in terms of 'sacrifice'.

SOMETIMES, AS AN EXHAUSTED PARENT, JUST TURNING UP AT CHURCH ON A SUNDAY IS A MAJOR ACT OF SACRIFICE AND THEREFORE AN ACT OF PRAISE!

But church also provides us with a spiritual momentum. We can be carried into a place of praise when we don't feel strong enough to get there by ourselves. Church is a family, sharing in life's ups and downs and helping each other through. Being with others who understand the joys and challenges we face is invaluable.

It's God's grace to us – to help us know Him in each season and keep us praising Him.

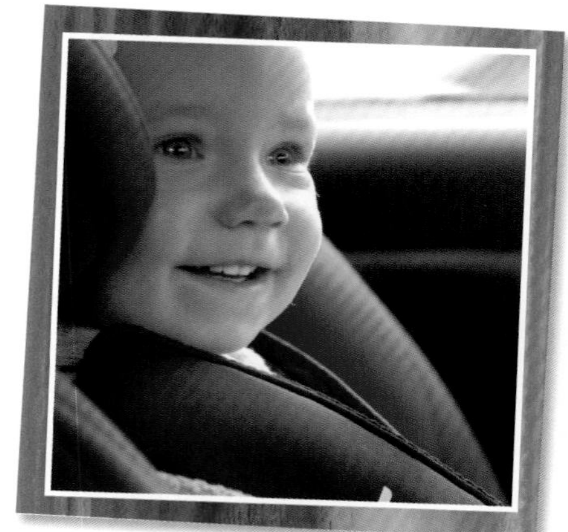

TIME TO ACT

1 In Philippians 4:4, Paul says that we should "rejoice in the Lord always". Take some time to reflect on what that means to you:

- **Rejoice** – Is this the same as feeling happy? Or does it have to do with thanking God for His promises to us, and trusting in Him?
- **In the Lord** – What are the things that God has given to us because of Jesus? What does that mean for us – in good times and in hard times?
- **Always** – Is there anything right now that is stopping you from praising God? Bring it to Him, confident that He is big enough to hold it – and you!

2 Think about people within your church community who may be going through a challenging time. Take time to commit them to God in prayer. Might God be asking you to provide practical support too?

TIME TO PRAY

Father God, thank you that whatever I go through, You are always with me.

Help me to keep praising You through the sunshine and the rain.

Amen.

BIG

ONLY GOT A MINUTE?

- In times of challenge or heartache it takes more emotional effort and commitment to praise God.
- Being part of a worshipping church community provides a spiritual rhythm to our lives.
- Being with others who understand the joys and challenges we face can help us to be carried into a place of praise when we don't feel strong enough to get there by ourselves.
- Is there anything right now that is stopping you from praising God? Bring it to Him and be confident that He is big enough to hold it – and you!

8 Praise God with everything I've got!

Psalm 146:2 (LWC)

I'm gonna praise God my whole life long! I'll sing to God for as long as I'm alive!

Do you have a favourite place you like to visit? Maybe it's your favourite park. Maybe it's your granny's house. Maybe it's somewhere far away, where you go for holidays. Our world is really BIG. It's bursting with exciting places to discover. And no matter how many places we've already been to, there's always more to see and explore!

It's like this with God. God is so BIG! His love is so big. And as we get bigger, we'll find there's much, much more to discover – about how amazing He is and how much He loves us. We've looked at some of the ways we can praise God. But that's just the beginning. **Learning to love and praise God is the adventure of a lifetime!**

TALK TOGETHER

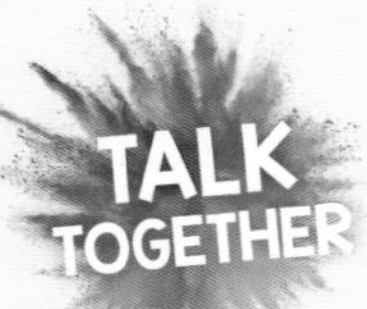

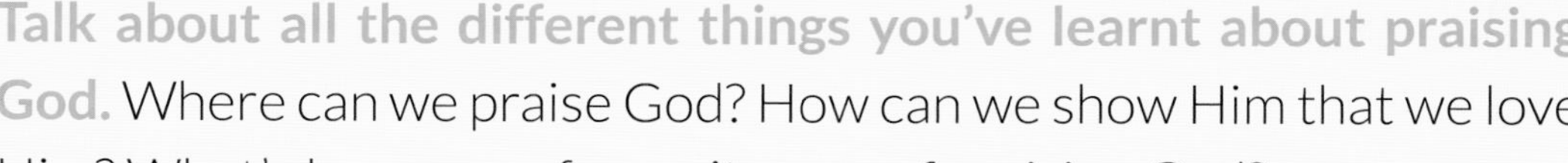

Talk about all the different things you've learnt about praising God. Where can we praise God? How can we show Him that we love Him? What's been your favourite way of praising God?

MAKE TOGETHER

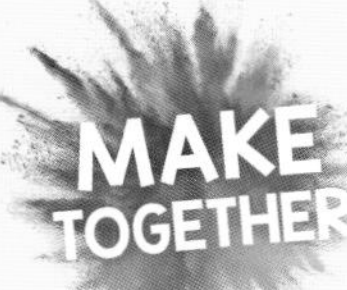

We can praise God all our life! Make a picture frame by getting a grown-up to cut out a rectangle on one side of an old cereal box. This makes your frame. Put stickers over the edge or paint your frame. Draw your favourite place to go inside.

PRAY TOGETHER

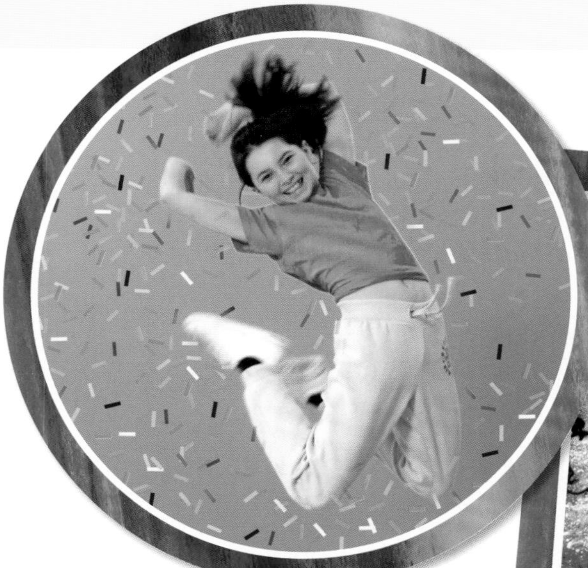

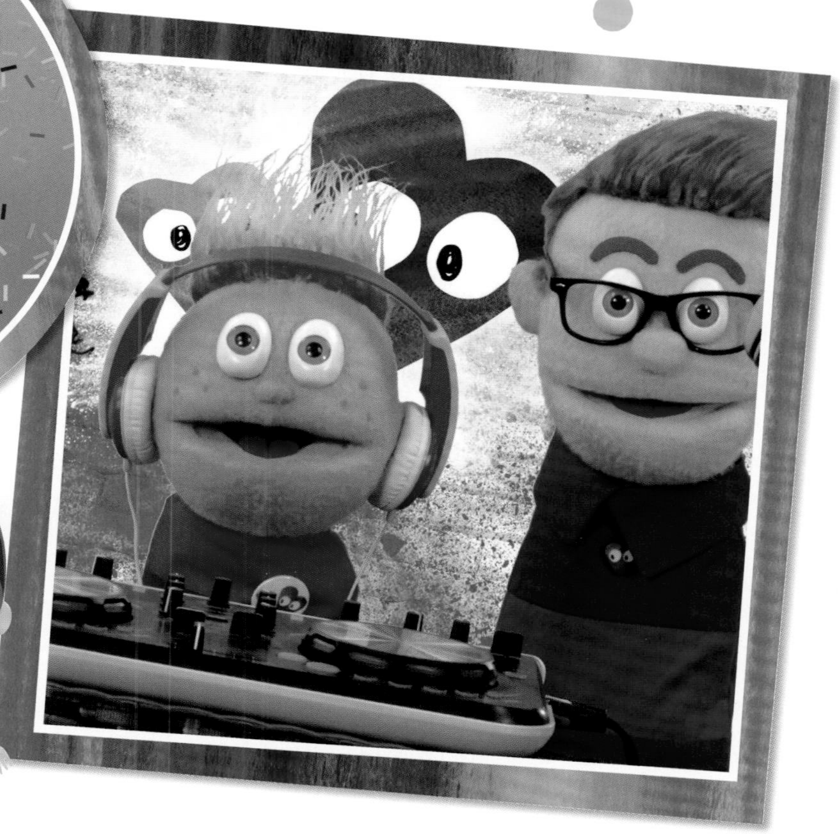

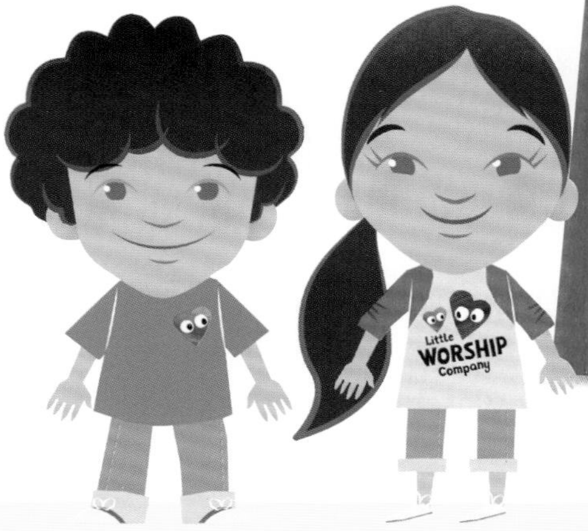

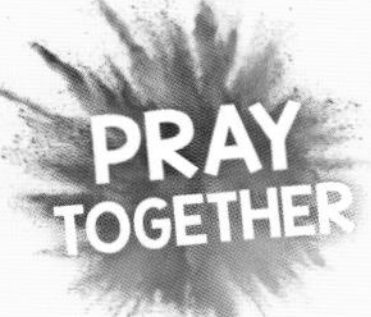

Dear God, **thank you that You are GREATER than I can imagine.** Thank you that Your love for me is BIGGER than I can imagine. Help me to keep on praising You my whole life long! **Amen.**

8 TIME TO REFLECT

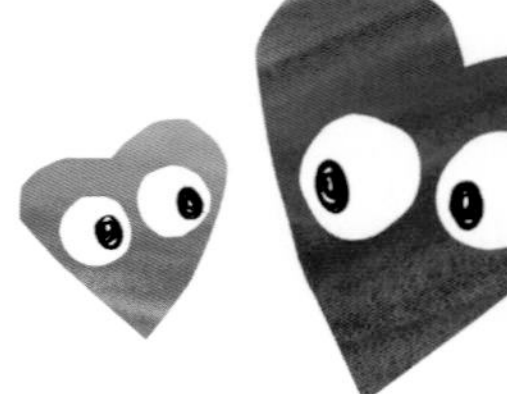

Psalm 146

Praise the Lord. Praise the Lord, my soul.
I will praise the Lord all my life; I will sing praise to my God as long as I live.
Do not put your trust in princes, in human beings, who cannot save.
When their spirit departs, they return to the ground;
on that very day their plans come to nothing.
Blessed are those whose help is the God of Jacob, whose hope is in the Lord their God.
He is the Maker of heaven and earth, the sea, and everything in them –
he remains faithful forever.
He upholds the cause of the oppressed and gives food to the hungry.
The Lord sets prisoners free, the Lord gives sight to the blind,
the Lord lifts up those who are bowed down, the Lord loves the righteous.
The Lord watches over the foreigner and sustains the fatherless and the widow,
but he frustrates the ways of the wicked.
The Lord reigns forever, your God, O Zion, for all generations.
Praise the Lord.

Psalm 146 is a song about commitment. It opens with a vow – the psalmist pledging to praise God for as long as life endures, and to make worship a lifetime endeavour. The invitation is there for us to do the same. The Bible gives us insights into what this looks like in practice. It's praising God quietly, when it's just us and God. It's praising God loudly in the congregation, with the sound of many voices and instruments. It's whispering praise to God at the many wonders we see around us each day. It's celebrating the good things God has given us and sharing them with others. It's trusting God when things are tough. And it's giving our lives to His service, committing ourselves to go where He leads and do all He asks.

This kind of vow isn't for the faint-hearted. As promises go, it's a big one. But at the heart of this psalm lies a much bigger promise – God's promise to us. If there's one thing that jumps out from Psalm 146, it's God's faithfulness.

WE WORSHIP THE GOD OF ETERNITY – WHO WAS THERE AT THE BEGINNING AND WILL REIGN FOR GENERATIONS TO COME.

And this same, majestic God of the universe cares deeply for all He has made. He hears our cries. He watches over the weakest and champions their cause. He is on our side. With Him, we cannot lose. As we walk with God day by day, season by season, we will learn and relearn His faithful love for us. And as we do, our praise will resound, not just throughout our lives, but as an echo throughout eternity.

TIME TO ACT

1 Create a 'map' of your journey with God, from the time you first committed to Him until now. Where have you walked with Him? What have been the faith landmarks along the way – the points where you saw God's faithfulness first-hand? Use this to praise Him.

2 Reflect on ways in which you can praise God each day as a family. For example, you might create a praise wall in the house. At a regular time each day, write up answers to prayer, something to be thankful for or words of love for God, and stick them to the wall. Write your thoughts and prayers in a family praise book.

TIME TO PRAY

Father God –

Nothing I could say, nothing I could do, could ever thank you enough for Your wonderful love and faithfulness.

But still I pray:

"Take my life and let it be consecrated, Lord, to thee.
Take my moments and my days.
Let them flow in ceaseless praise."
(Frances Ridley Havergal)

Amen.

BIG

ONLY GOT A MINUTE?

- In Psalm 146, the psalmist pledges to praise God for as long as life endures, and to make worship a lifetime endeavour.
- We worship the God of eternity, who was there at the beginning and will reign for generations to come.
- This majestic, eternal God is forever for us. He is on our side. With Him, we cannot lose.
- What is your map of your journey with God? From the time you first committed to Him until now, where have you walked with Him? When have you seen God's faithfulness first-hand?

Crafts and recipes

DEVOTION 2 PAPER WINDMILL

You will need:

- Split pin
- Square of paper
- Straw
- Plasticine or sticky tack
- Pencil

1. Fold your square of paper in half to make two triangles, unfold and fold the other way. You will now have a piece of paper with two diagonal folds.
2. Let your child decorate both sides of the paper with crayons.
3. Cut along each of the diagonal lines, from the corners to two-thirds to the centre.
4. Fold the four corner sections down to the centre of the paper, holding each section under your thumb at the centre as you work.
5. Once all four triangles are in place, put a blob of plasticine on top. With a very sharp pencil, pierce through all the layers to make a hole that you can then thread a split pin through.
6. Open the split pin and grip it around the top of a straw. You will need to work your windmill around a few times to make sure it moves smoothly.

DEVOTION 1

Potato stamping

DEVOTION 3

Home-made musical instruments

DEVOTION 4

Feet painting

DEVOTION 6 LOVE BUG BISCUITS

You will need:

- 200g (8oz) butter, softened
- 200g (8oz) sugar
- 1 large egg
- ½ tsp vanilla extract
- 400g (16oz) plain flour, plus extra for dusting
- Icing sugar
- Food colouring
- Edible eyes
- Rolling pin
- Heart-shaped cutter

1. Preheat oven to 200°C/180°C fan/ gas mark 6 and grease or line a baking sheet.
2. Mix the butter and sugar by hand or with an electric mixer.
3. Add the egg and vanilla.
4. Add the flour to make a dough. If the dough feels a bit sticky, add a little bit more flour.
5. Once you have a dough, roll it out with a rolling pin so it is about 1cm thick.
6. Cut biscuits out into heart shapes and put on the baking sheet.
7. Put in the oven to cook for 8-10 minutes.
8. Mix icing sugar with water and food colouring to make a thick paste.
9. When cool, ice biscuits and add edible eyes.

DEVOTION 5

Thankfulness peacock

DEVOTION 7

Paper chains and bunting

DEVOTION 8

Cereal box picture frame

Praise Party

thank you prayers

Thank you, God, for praise parties!

Thank you for my great friends.

Thank you that I can dance.

Thank you that I can jump up high.

Thank you for my crazy arms.

Thank you for music that makes me spin.

Thank you for my swinging hips.

Thank you that I can praise You.

Thank you for my clapping hands.

Thank you, God, for my little worship time!

Amen.

Also available from

The **Little Worship Company** offers a range of inspiring products, including DVDs, an app **(Little Worship Company World)**, devotionals, curriculums and books. Our products are filled with beautifully-produced worship videos, prayers, games, stories and Bible quotes.

Each DVD follows a devotional journey, teaching your child timeless Bible truths. The DVDs and app have been created to help adults and children to discover God together at home, at church or out in the community.

 **info@littleworshipcompany.com**  **Littleworshipcompany**  **@littleworshipcompany**

Little Worship Company World

Worship anytime, anywhere

Through our digital world, hosted by the entertaining **Looyah family**, you and your child will be taken on a journey through beautifully-produced worship videos, games, stories, Bible quotes and age-appropriate studies. Each week there will be a new exciting journey of content to explore, as you and your little one discover God together.

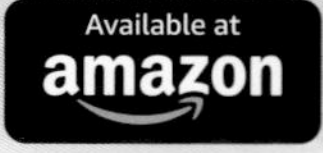

Apple, the Apple logo and iPad are trademarks of Apple Inc., registered in the U.S. and other countries and regions. App Store is a service mark of Apple Inc. Google Play and the Google Play logo are trademarks of Google LLC. Amazon's trademark is used under license from Amazon.com, Inc. or its affiliates.